Listen Up!

UNLOCKING THE SECRET LANGUAGES OF INTUITIVES, CREATIVES AND ANALYTICAL THINKERS

AMY LANCI

Listen Up!
Unlocking the Secret Languages of Intuitives, Creatives, and Analytical Thinkers

Print ISBN: 979-8-218-01246-5
Ebook ISBN: 979-8-218-00915-1
Library of Congress Control Number: 2022922874

Printed in the United States

Contents

This book is dedicated to my family, my friends, and to all those who believed in my gifts way before I ever did. Thank you for helping me to feel heard.

Introduction

I was a child of no words. People scared me. The world was terrifying. Loud noises were too much. With no way to call for help, I clung to safety as best as I could, and, at the time, my sole source of comfort was my family. I considered everyone else off-limits.

My internal world was all about protection and retreat. To the external world, I was a very socially awkward and needy child.

After I tested negative for autism, the doctors chalked up my behavior to my speech delay and sent me on my way to get speech therapy for the next nine years. Over time, words finally escaped my lips, and I started to trust other kids enough to form friendships. Even then, I still felt very different than everyone else around me. Deep inside, I felt like there was a hidden truth that lurked, crawling its way around my thoughts silently as I went about my life, leaving me with more questions than answers.

Eventually, I found solace in writing. The written word allowed me to freely articulate my emotions and my ideas without the interference of worldly judgments and rules. It was in this space I was able to recount my day, explore different worlds, and play within the confines of my mind. At some point, I created my own superhero—a play on Marvel Comics' "The Phoenix"—but made her my own. It was glorious, and I loved it. Yet there were moments of sadness and loneliness because I still felt far removed from the truth of my being, which felt so separate from my external world.

Everyone around me saw me as the typical sweet Asian American girl who got good grades and did anything and everything to make her family proud. I felt extremely misunderstood and uncomfortable in my skin.

Then my life took a turn. After a fateful trip to a Baja research station through the local community college (I was a sophomore in high school), I changed all my other plans to become a journalist and beelined to marine biology. I got my bachelor of science in ecology, behavior, and evolution from the University of California, San Diego. I worked as a lab technician contracted for the National Marine Fisheries Service. For fourteen years, my primary role was to extract the DNA from sea turtle tissue samples (e.g., skin, blood, dead turtle embryos, and muscle) and turn it into data that would eventually play a role in protecting sea turtles under the Endangered Species Act. In a nutshell, the work I did helped scientists determine whether or not a fishery was catching too many sea turtles. If so, they could shut the fishery down. (To this day, every time I tell the story about my prior career, I get a little embarrassed because I have no clue how to describe my work succinctly!)

All in all, life was good. My time in the lab was mixed with some fun adventures. How many people can say they caught and sampled turtles in San Diego and the US Virgin Islands? My bet is not many!

As cool as my research was, I still felt stifled. My internal truth would not let me forget that there was something I was not seeing. I felt this way despite falling in love, getting married, overcoming some major health issues, and doing some serious work on myself emotionally and physically. What more could there be to unfold?

When I got the news that my then-lab manager was leaving us to become a health coach, the change in personnel seemed to spur me into action. I thought that perhaps going into business for myself would shed some light on this "unknowingness" that refused to go away.

I completed a year-long health coaching certification program. Despite my best efforts, I still could not make a dime from my coaching business. I was a new mom (my daughter was born one month after I got my certification) and had no idea what I was doing. Marketing? Charging money? Business felt alien to me. What on earth was I supposed to do?

After a lot of trial and error and thousands of dollars spent, my business coach saw how my lack of progress had left me feeling emotionally raw and demoralized. It was then she challenged me to change my business focus to copywriting. I seemed to have a natural knack for the written word. I also saw a clearer view of how my craft could fit inside a business model.

Lo and behold, I got my first two clients within one week of changing over my website and business cards. Hallelujah!

As things unfolded, I saw two distinct benefits to this new direction. It defined a clear deliverable to an audience that was willing to pay. It combined the creative and analytical parts of me. It was a much easier sell than health coaching, and my confidence skyrocketed

I started to notice something I had never pieced together. When I shifted my focus to writing, my clients opened up to me on a deeper level. Some of them said things they had never spoken out loud before. Some of them saw their value in a way they had never seen before. Some even started to cry during the consultations. I started to notice I had a gift for pulling people's stories out of them. What was even more profound was that this didn't start when I became a copywriter. This was an innate ability that had been with me since birth, and I was finally owning up to it.

As I was helping my clients own new parts of themselves, I went on a similar journey with them. This was when I really dove into my spirituality. I started reading material about empaths (people who feel empathy for others to the point of taking on other people's emotions as their own). I had to own up to another fundamental truth: I was an empath myself.

It all suddenly made sense. My behavior as a child. The feeling of "not belonging." All the times getting "lost" in others. The need to protect myself. I thought it was just people-pleasing, but it wasn't. I even recall instances when I was fine one moment, then angry the next—for no other reason than sitting right next to someone who most likely felt those feelings. Unexplained bodily pains were no longer an enigma because they, too, were a side effect of my empathic nature. The shadow lurking in the darkness had finally stepped into the light—and an undiscovered part of myself began to emerge. I saw a vision of a beautiful phoenix waiting to soar the skies.

Now, why did I tell you my story? Why bother spending the time going over all of this with you when you just want to dive in and get what you need from this book? I'm using my own story to model the framework this book will lay out for you.

My journey allowed me to dive into the analytical (the scientist), the creative (the writer), and the intuitive (the empath) aspects of my total Self. My journey has not only deepened my self-awareness but also revealed three primary groups of people who naturally resonate with me and my work. By focusing my efforts on learning to speak the language of these three personas,

I have been able to jump between worlds and translate different worldviews. Even though the three groups are made of fundamentally different people, they all want the same thing: to be seen and heard as they truly are without shame and judgment.

If you can give people the gift of being heard, then not only will you earn their trust but you will earn their respect too. Whether you are working to hone your personal elevator pitch for a particular audience or trying to engage with a coworker who thinks very differently than you, this book will come in handy.

I'm ready when you are. Are you coming?

How To Use This Book

Let me make this abundantly clear: This book is not meant to typecast intuitives, creatives, or analytical thinkers—or anyone, really. The moment we put an individual or a group of people in a category, we start to look at them with immediate judgment based on surface-level observations and rumors. That's not the point of this book. In fact, every person on this planet is going to walk the line with one, two, or even all three of these groups.

My intention for this book is to teach people how to better communicate with and earn the trust of those with the same or opposing mindsets. Whether you are an intuitive person who wants to connect with more members of the intuitive community, or you are a creative business owner who is trying to engage and earn the respect of an audience of critical thinkers, such as attorneys or doctors, this book is for you.

Now, I'm not asking you to engage in "people-pleasing" or allowing the voices of others to speak louder than your own. Instead, look at this book as a mirror to reflect back what you see in others and what others see in you.

If you are a changemaker and your eyes are set on creating real change, then you can't afford to view life and people in a black-and-white, matter-of-fact way. You need to be able to live in a world of gray where the typical rules of "right and wrong" no longer apply, where walls are torn down, and all that is left is the space between you and other people. You don't need to be everyone's friend, and not everyone needs to be yours. You just need to be willing to understand—or at least to try.

Keep your ears to the ground and open up your heart. We all speak different languages, but we all desire to be heard.

As your eyes gaze upon the words in this book, think about the people in your life you wish to better understand. What do you personally need to know in order to deepen the relationship? What do you wish for them to know about you, and what words do you need in order to accurately get your point across but still hold their attention? Most importantly, what insights are you willing to receive from this book in regard to who you are and what you really want?

We live in a world where division is the norm and compassion is the diamond in the rough. Let's change that around.

Intuitive Healers

"As long as it serves the Highest Good."

INSIDER'S LOOK

Intuitive healers, otherwise known as the "woo woo" crowd, are a specialized population of people who are deeply in tune with their intuition and have studied different healing and spiritual modalities in order to discover the truth behind their spiritual gifts; they fully realize the reason why they were born. Their main driver and motivator is to pursue the Highest Good of all. In other words, if they do something they believe will help themselves and others in the process, they will feel they have played their role in the path laid out by the Divine.

The Intuitive crowd tends to borrow spiritual and philosophical principles from The Old World (ancient Egypt, Greece, Wiccan) and mainstream religion (such as Buddhism, Wicca, or Christianity). Intuitives like to put their own spin on religion, incorporating such modalities as Jungian psychology, "The Law of Attraction" (introduced by Abraham Hicks), and mind-body-spirit medicine (inspired by the work of Louise Hay). Even an old system like the tarot has been made more accessible and user-friendly in the form of derivatives like Oracle cards and Angel cards. Intuitives also gravitate toward tools such as the Bible, astrology, I-Ching, Ayurveda, the chakra system, and Feng Shui.

Oftentimes, this crowd refers to the physical plane as "3D" and the spiritual realm as "5D." To further illustrate what these are, here is an example: Imagine walking down the street as you normally would, and you decide to stop in front of a shop window to admire the clothes on the mannequins. All of a sudden, your spirit leaves your body, and now you're watching yourself staring at the shop window as if you're a member of the audience. Think of 5D as a way to see what can't be present in the 3D realm. That's why you'll hear experts who can see auras or blocked chakras and those who astral project say they see in the 5D. It's like you're looking at the world from the vantage point of an eagle, soaring through the skies and observing the miniature people and towns below.

Intuitive healers love diving deep within themselves. Sometimes this is in the form of shadow work, confronting old wounds and traumas. An intuitive healer will often undertake a journey of self-discovery with the assistance of another intuitive healer gifted in the ways of Akashic Records and past-life regressions. Perhaps the most surface-level of the journey to Self is discovering, confronting, and accepting one's unique spiritual gifts. For instance, a clairaudient hears intuitive messages (either in conversation with someone or directly from Spirit), while a clairvoyant sees visions of the future. Keep in mind that each individual can have many spiritual gifts, and each gift is a milestone of self-discovery.

STRENGTHS OF INTUITIVES

WELL-BEING AND SELF-AWARENESS AT THE FOREFRONT

Intuitive healers are well-versed and passionate about well-being. They know that the word "health" is not isolated to just the physical body but also applies to the mental, emotional, and spiritual aspects of a person. In fact, they see physical and mental ailments as symptoms of emotional and spiritual issues. This is what they call the "spirit-mind-body connection." For instance, a weight issue may be rooted in emotional eating, and emotional eating is rooted in childhood trauma. Intuitive healers know that when the root cause is addressed, it will positively affect the underlying conditions.

There is no need to explain the importance of diving deep when it comes to inner growth and continuous evolution. In fact, this population lives and breathes transformation. Ever heard of the saying, "Let go of what no longer serves you"? This is what it is all about! Intuitive healers are all about becoming aware of past wounds (from this lifetime and the last) and then going forth to do whatever it takes to heal. Some of the most prescribed ways to address these wounds are prayer, meditation, journaling, oracle and tarot cards, therapy, Reiki, and shamanism.

STRONG DESIRE TO MAKE THE WORLD A BETTER PLACE FOR ALL

Intuitive healers have an inherent need to greatly change the world. Remember what I said about "serving the Highest Good of All?" Yep! This is definitely when it comes into play. Intuitive healers have been through a lot on their life journey (who hasn't, though, right?), and their experiences have influenced them in a way where they want to save people from the same fate. Or they were inspired by something on their path and realized they had a real gift, then were even more inspired to share this gift. Helping others is an absolute strength for intuitive healers.

SOUL MISSION AS THEIR NORTH STAR

Their conviction to seek truth, light, and their purpose is unparalleled. In fact, many of them may already have a good sense of why they were placed here on this earth, which makes them determined to dive deep and discover the deeper truths within their hearts, minds, and souls. Even if they resist certain truths along the way, they eventually see the value of accepting these truths when they keep presenting themselves time and time again.

For myself, I was always getting the message that I was meant to walk the line and serve as both an educator and healer in this world. I rejected this truth because I didn't feel worthy of such a task, and I didn't like ambiguity and vagueness around my purpose. Walk the line? Really? I reasoned that maybe if I waited long enough, I'd fall on one side of the line or the other. Then I'd know if I was meant to be a healer or an educator. Maybe the choice could be made for me. Over and over again, I saw signs that the more I embraced the truth, the more opportunities opened up.

Stories like mine are pretty common in the community. The soul mission presents itself and serves as a North Star to recalibrate our wayward ships when we get lost at sea.

POWERFUL WHEN FULLY IN TOUCH WITH THEIR SPIRITUAL GIFTS

I used to be a skeptic of anything having to do with God, the supernatural, and anything I couldn't see with my own eyes. When I heard of people with abilities such as speaking with spirits, hearing other people's thoughts, or healing the sickness of others simply by shifting the energy, I slowly backed away and minded my own business. It was hard for me to grasp what was possible metaphysically when I couldn't even grapple with and accept my own abilities, let alone understand what others were capable of.

But at this point in my life, I have worked with some of the world's most masterful healers who have shown me things I could not deny or look away from. Without going down a rabbit hole, I will say this: When I meet people who are fully in touch with their gifts and use them properly with the world, amazing and miraculous things happen. They are the embodiment of what it truly means to be within their purpose and own every inch of who they are. When you meet the Real McCoys, watch and study them. You may be surprised as to what you learn!

CHALLENGES FOR THIS POPULATION

Although intuitives do their best to stay in a grounded place of enlightenment, they are still vulnerable to the human condition with strife and shadows to overcome.

Before approaching intuitive healers to engage in conversation or talk to them as a community, here are some challenges they experience with the world at large or within their population on a day-to-day basis.

COMPETING MODALITIES AND PHILOSOPHIES

As strange as it sounds, I have seen members of the intuitive healer community advocate for the "abundance mindset, no need for competition, we are all in this together." I have also seen modalities compete with each other. Sometimes competition takes the form of who is more "enlightened" or "awakened," which is based on ego and life philosophy (aka those who have stayed humble versus those who have grown arrogant). At other times, people compete based on the strength of spiritual gifts measured by how "sensitive" an individual is to the energies floating around a situation or environment or how many gifts someone has (I have seen people list as many as twenty to thirty gifts in a group forum just to share for the sake of sharing). I've even seen it where different practitioners will question why a potential client will pick one modality over another and be extremely critical of the chosen practitioner.

Keep in mind, all competition between intuitives, regardless of how dysfunctional the behavior, ultimately seeks to bring integrity to "serving the Highest Good."

RESISTANCE TO THE CONCRETE AND PRACTICAL

Many members of the intuitive community love answering the question of WHY things happen and WHY they need to continue on the path they need to be on. However, the HOW can trip up intuitives, especially when the HOW involves concrete action steps that may be devoid of fun and lead to uncomfortable situations.

Here is an example: Let's say someone wants a dream house. They love talking about it, imagining the layout of the house, and even creating a vision board to bring it to life. This is something they've wanted for their entire lives. However, they need money to get that dream house, and that money needs to come from marketing and making sales in their business. The idea of being seen or asking for too much money may trigger past wounds around these issues. Instead of working on these issues simultaneously with the action steps (like marketing and sales), they will retreat and seek more healing while holding their vision board tight to them.

Even the language around practical steps can meet resistance. Before I left my job as a scientist, I wanted to revel in the colorful language of my creative and intuitive sides as much as I could when I wasn't working on science. It was refreshing and very freeing. As my desire to leave my job grew, the more I looked at "scientist speak" as chains to hold me down and keep me suppressed. Now that I am a full-time entrepreneur, I use my "scientist speak" freely and find it quite fun because I no longer have a negative association with my scientist self.

If you are trying to strike up a conversation with someone from the intuitive community and plan to keep it to very concrete and practical topics, make sure it is a topic that directly applies to their life. It's not that they don't want to understand you or want to engage (in fact, I've met many intuitives who have a strong science background), but you stand to lose their attention or awaken their demons if you don't create a safe middle ground.

CONFLICT BETWEEN THEIR NEED TO HELP OTHERS AND THEIR DESIRE FOR WEALTH

Truthfully, you don't need much to live your life. Maybe a place to live, clothing, a car to drive, and enough money to keep food on the table and keep the lights on. But you know that there are so many more opportunities to experience the world, try new things, and help others when you have more wealth at your disposal.

I see intuitive healers acknowledge everything I mentioned above and yet feel internally conflicted about their desire for wealth. Perhaps it is due to the philosophy of the "Highest Good," as that implies the benefits to the collective and money is often represented as a benefit to the individual. Perhaps it's because they just want to help people and not ask for anything in return.

For some, it is because of past dealings with snake-oil practitioners—charlatans who pose as practitioners in order to steal money. These victims who go on to become healers themselves often feel like they need to "make up" for the trail of travesty left by the snake oil practitioners by offering their services for an extremely low price.

This is what you have to understand: A healer's life purpose and need to help people is what drives them. Money is a means to the end.

STILL HAVE A HARD TIME ACCEPTING WHO THEY ARE . . . IN PUBLIC

Many have had a history of hiding their intuitive gifts out of fear of sounding crazy or receiving shame, especially those who grew up with a strong religious or scientific upbringing and were condemned for their gifts. To find acceptance again, they tucked their gifts away within them, waiting for a time when they would be free to finally explore them.

Some are in some kind of state of denial, which ranges from not talking about intuition or spirituality at all to full-on condemning others for being "out of the intuitive closet." A lot of times, what people say out loud is a reflection of how they really feel about themselves—a mirror of their inner state rather than an appraisal of others.

Even when intuitives fully accept their gifts, they have a hard time being taken seriously by those who are scientific, non-religious, and non-spiritual thinkers—or non-believers in general. If they have a core wound around acceptance or recognition, they are more likely to keep their intuitive gifts silent when speaking with an individual or crowd who is not part of the community.

OFTEN GET LOST IN PERSONAL GROWTH AND
LOSE SIGHT OF THEIR MISSION

For many intuitives, they have a deep need and desire to go deeper and deeper into the mysteries of their soul with the intention of figuring out how they tick and what that has to do with their purpose in life. While personal development is extremely helpful for diving into past wounds and kickstarting some much-needed healing, it can often go to the extreme. I have seen people go from one modality to another, reaching for past lives and drumming up visions of the future. If you think about it, searching within ourselves can be the greatest rabbit hole we can ever go down. I have seen people get so lost in figuring out who they are that they end up spending more time lost in this quandary rather than moving forward with their projects. "What am I supposed to do?" becomes a distraction as opposed to leading them closer to where they need to go.

WHAT THE CONVERSATION STARTER NEEDS TO KEEP IN MIND

GET A GOOD GRASP OF THE LANGUAGE BY LIGHTLY STUDYING HEALING MODALITIES.

To learn the language of this community, you need to be willing to wear the hat of a lifelong spiritual learner. Think of a monk studying in a temple hidden away in the mountains. In the morning, the monk is paying attention to any lessons that fall into his lap as he does his daily chores. In the afternoon, the monk will rotate between reading sacred scrolls and mentoring under the tutelage of his elders. By sundown, he is reflecting on everything that happened that day and takes a moment to apply all of it to the deeper truth embedded inside of his spirit, sitting there in wonderment at the divine design of life.

In other words, it is not enough to learn a glossary of definitions to engage with this crowd. You need to understand the significance behind these terms, where they really come from, and why people truly care about these concepts. Let's take the chakra system, for instance. The chakra system is a structure of channels and portals within our body that allows divine energy to flow within us constantly. While that is a good bite-sized piece of information, it doesn't give a good indication as to why the chakra system is trusted and used by so many.

Now, if you researched deeper into the chakra system, you'd find out that there are seven chakras, and each one is the epicenter of a key emotion. Once a chakra is blocked, then that epicenter of energy is trapped and can affect the individual emotionally, mentally, physically, and spiritually. For example, if your solar plexus (the part around your belly button that represents personal power) is blocked, then your sense of personal authority is compromised, and it is hard to gather the inner strength to stand up for yourself.

When it comes to learning the language of intuitive healers, take some time to study different healing modalities just to get an idea as to where these terms come from and their significance to the population.

DON'T MIX THE CONCEPTS OF "RELIGION" AND "SPIRITUALITY."

Whether you are a spiritual person who doesn't belong to a religion or a religious person who associates spirituality with the church—or some hybrid of both—it doesn't matter. What matters most is that you distinguish religion from spirituality because it will make a world of difference in your conversations with an intuitive healer.

Here is a good way to distinguish the two: Religion has everything to do with a set belief system followed by a group of people, while spirituality is all about the individual and what they believe to be true from their own experiences, regardless of religion or upbringing.

There are common concepts spoken of in the intuitive healer space, but it doesn't necessarily mean all of them follow these concepts or believe for them to be true. Instead, it is from the standpoint of studying where you feel led to go, seeing if it rings true when you apply it to your own life, and then forming your own opinion about said concept—which goes back to the concept of spirituality as an individual journey.

So, keep in mind, anytime you talk about religion and spirituality with anyone (even if they are not an intuitive healer), it will greatly impact the conversation depending on which path you go down. When you converse on the topic of spirituality, for instance, you're speaking as two individuals with your own unique sense of what spirituality is. When you're speaking about religion, you and your conversation partner are speaking as representatives of the religion, whether you realize it or not. Just remember this as it may explain why religion can be a tense topic to talk about, but spirituality has more room to play with.

INTUITION GOES BY DIFFERENT NAMES BASED ON SPIRITUAL AND RELIGIOUS FOUNDATIONS.

Believe it or not, the concept of intuition goes by many different names and titles depending on someone's spiritual and religious beliefs. For instance, the New Age community may use terms such as "messages from the Divine" or "downloads." However, if you use these terms around someone with a Christian foundation or background, it might confuse them or turn them off. Instead, terms such as "faith' or "Spirit" would have a deeper meaning. Then there are those who are on "neutral" ground. They acknowledge their intuitive abilities but are pretty open to all kinds of terminology, theories, and beliefs.

Therefore, it is important to see where someone is at with their religious and spiritual beliefs in order to figure out which words to use when conversing on the topic of intuition.

THIS CROWD LIVES BETWEEN TWO WORLDS.

The thoughts and mindsets of strongly spiritual-minded people can often be stuck up in the ether/5D, and it is hard to come back to earth. In other words, with this crowd, it is easier to discuss or develop philosophical and spiritual concepts or messages, but they may enjoy this part so much it is hard to get them to apply the practical or describe what they are experiencing in layman's terms. This often stems from the need to create the world they want/need, which is often very different from the world we live in. As a result, they continue to live "in-between" both worlds as they go about life, wondering when they will fully wake up to their true selves as divine creators.

RECOMMENDED COMMUNICATION STRATEGIES

The following is a list of communication strategies to try out in order to open doors, earn trust, and find commonality between yourself and someone in the intuitive healing space (whether you are a fellow member of the same community or not). Try any of these in conversations in person and in virtual spaces.

FIGURE OUT WHAT STAGE THEY ARE ON THEIR JOURNEY.

When it comes to their spiritual gifts, every intuitive is within the following four stages of self-acceptance. Understanding what stage they are in will allow you to gauge how much you need to reassure them that they are in a safe space with you.

THE FOUR STAGES:

DENIAL

Never explored their spiritual gifts but secretly suspected it (like a dirty secret). Often due to upbringing.

IN THE CLOSET

Have started to read and research spiritual modalities and pieced together their experiences and gifts. But won't mention it unless they are in "safe" company.

OUT IN THE OPEN

They have no problem talking about their beliefs and their spiritual gifts for the world to see. But they compartmentalize this part of themselves from what they do for a living.

FULL-BLOWN WOO

Actively uses their spiritual gifts in their career/ business and brings them to every conversation.

NARROW THEM DOWN TO ANY OF THE TOP THREE PERSPECTIVES.

To slice it down more, here are three perspectives to look out for:

STATE OF BEING: "I AM INTUITIVE."

In other words, this is a descriptive term to define a characteristic of the person in question.

WHO THEY ARE: "I AM AN INTUITIVE."

In this case, the person is identifying themselves as someone who has an extraordinarily sharp intuition, as if it is part of their identity.

COUPLED WITH SPIRITUALITY VS. RELIGION – "I AM A PROPHET/FAITH-BASED/HEALER."

Similar to the person whose identity hinges on their intuition, people in this category go one step further and intertwine their spirituality/religion to further define their intuitive abilities.

FIND OUT HOW PEOPLE CATEGORIZE THEMSELVES.

Based on someone's spiritual and religious foundations and beliefs, you will have to use different words for each individual in order to keep them engaged and prevent them from tuning out.

FAITH-BASED

- Faith
- Spirit or Holy Spirit
- Prophet
- Prophetic words

INTUITIVE (SUSPECT)

- Empathic
- Emotionally sensitive
- Feel for others
- Downloads
- Messages

INTUITIVE (EXPERIENCED)

- Blessings
- Clearing space
- Grounding
- Divine timing

Compare notes on spiritual tools and practices.

If you have ever dabbled in any spiritual tools, this is the crowd to throw this out to. Think of it as the equivalent of "comparing notes" or "trading baseball cards." Behind each tool and practice is a story of what led you and your conversation partner to try these tools and why you do or don't continue using them.

Spiritual tools and practices include but are not limited to divination cards (Tarot, Oracle, Angel, and Goddess), numerology, astrology, Human Design, chakra clearings, feng shui, qigong, Reiki, clearing space with sage, essential oils, and meditation.

The Law of Attraction

The Law of Attraction (LOA) is a concept that is widely touted and spoken of in the intuitive space, made famous by Abraham Hicks. The basic concept of LOA is this: We all have the power of the Divine within us, and once we tap into that power, we can create and manifest what we desire (e.g., money, soulmates, opportunities). Whether you read the book or not, this is an interesting concept to read CliffNotes on and engage in conversation.

HAY HOUSE

Hay House is a global publisher and retailer of personal development products that include books, oracle and tarot cards, meditation CDs, and online courses. Topics covered range from relationships, wealth manifestation, confidence, and even modern-day witchcraft.

Hay House was created by the highly regarded Louise Hay and continues on today after her death as the "go-to" source for everything mentioned above. If you happen to follow Hay House, a good conversation starter could be, "Hey, did you hear about Hay House's latest sale? You can get some oracle decks for as little as nine dollars!" This tactic only works if you are a genuine Hay House follower because it is the excitement of the sale that drives the conversation. Without that, it completely falls flat.

SELF-CARE ROUTINES

Do you follow a certain routine every day to take care of yourself? Or are you looking to explore new ways to relax and relieve stress? Now is the time to talk about that! As I mentioned before, the intuitive crowd is fully aware of the consequences of running your body and spirit into the ground. This means that self-care routines such as meditation, nature walks, journaling, expressing gratitude, massages, healthy diets, and exercise regimes are all great door openers!

Then, depending on who you are, who you are talking to, and what your belief system is, you may even want to speak on topics such as grounding, divine timing, and the art of release and surrender.

GET VULNERABLE

When you've built up enough trust or rapport, talk about what you really want and what resistance you are experiencing spiritually (e.g., "The messages I have been receiving have been telling me to go one way, but then I get triggered and resist. Then I'm stuck again.") When you can talk about this part of yourself, you create a space where judgment has no power, and you're essentially inviting the other person to join you.

If your conversation partner reciprocates, then you can potentially talk about the afterlife, spiritual experiences (like divine interventions, messages from angels, talking to dead loved ones), or honoring ancestors. You can relate this to healing generational wounds and other forms of healing to discover self-love, get closer to the Divine, and realize your life purpose.

KEYWORDS AND KEY PHRASES

3D (OR THIRD DIMENSION)
This refers to the physical plane. If you are reading this book right now, you are most definitely living in the third dimension!

5D (OR FIFTH DIMENSION)
The spiritual plane where people can tap into their Higher Selves, Angels, and Spirit Guides

ABUNDANCE
The position or the state of being where resources such as joy and wealth are always readily available

AKASHIC RECORDS

The sacred spiritual library where all information in the universe is stored. This is typically accessed through deep spiritual meditation or through specifically trained experts.

ANCESTRAL WOUNDS

Also referred to as "generational wounds," these are wounds that are carried from one generation to another until it is resolved.

ASTROLOGY

The study of people and world events based on birth dates and the movement of the stars and planets

AYURVEDA

Developed in India over 3,000 years ago, Ayurveda has served as one of the oldest holistic healing systems on the planet. In the New World, this practice is typically categorized as "alternative medicine." Ayurveda looks at the connection between physical health with mind, heart, and spirit. There are five elements that are widely used in this practice: space, air, fire, water, and earth.[1]

---

1   Katie Miller, "What is Ayurveda?" March 20, 2021, https://www.webmd.com/balance/guide/ayurvedic-treatments#1.

BLOCKED CHAKRAS

When unresolved emotions, wounds, and issues are trapped in any of the main seven chakras, compromising and preventing the natural flow of divine energy. Blocked chakras are at the root of mental, emotional, and physical health issues.

BURNING SAGE

The act of burning a stick of dried sacred ceremonial sage to clear unwanted energies and entities from a space (aka your home). This practice dates back to prehistoric times, and some version exists all over the world. The sage used for this practice is not your average use-at-home herb; it is the California White Sage.

CHAKRAS

A series of portals and channels within the human body where divine energy enters and exits constantly. Without these chakras, we would cease to exist. When one or more chakras experience "blocks" (see definition of Blocked Chakras) or "interferences," imbalances in physical, mental, emotional, or spiritual health occur.

Without further ado, here are the main seven chakras[2] to keep in mind:

The Crown
Location: Top of the head

Represents: Divine connection to Self, others, and the universe

The Third Eye
Location: In the middle of the forehead

Represents: Intuition, imagination, and sensing future events (only for those who are very in tune with their third eye)

The Throat
Location: The throat (pretty straightforward)

Represents: Communication and expression through words

The Heart
Location: In the chest

---

2   Sara Lindberg, "What Are The 7 Chakras and How Can You Unblock Them?" August 24, 2020, https://www.healthline.com/health/what-are-chakras#the-7-main-chakras.

Represents: Emotions, namely love and compassion

The Solar Plexus
Location: In the stomach area

Represents: Confidence, stability, security, personal control, and power

The Sacral
Location: Right below the belly button

Represents: Sexual and creative energy

The Root
Location: Base of spine

Represents: The foundation for stability and security. This is the area that helps you feel grounded.

CHURCH HURT
When one experiences shame, guilt, anger, sadness, or frustration within the confines of their church

CLAIRAUDIENT
Someone who hears divine messages

CLAIRVOYANT
Someone who sees people, places, and events in their dreams before they become reality

CLAIRSENTIENT
Someone who senses people and the environment with their intuitive abilities. For instance, they may get a sense that someone is lying or sense something is off

THE COLLECTIVE
The entire human race

CORD-CUTTING
The act of removing attachments to events, emotions, and people from the past

CORDS
Attachments to events, people, and emotions of the past, whether good or bad

DIVINE TIMING
The idea that things will happen when they are intended. In other words, you have free will (see definition) to make your choices, but if you are not

getting the things you desire despite how much you wish for it, they will come at just the right time. Sometimes a lesson needs to be learned. Sometimes other pieces need to snap into place first, without your knowing. Divine timing is all about allowing for things to line up in their own time, and whenever that is will work out for the Highest Good of all.

DOWNLOADS

A sudden thought, idea, message, or revelation gifted from the Divine that encompasses important lessons and answers to the person who received the download. Please note: Downloads always show up in someone's mind, as they are "downloaded from the Divine."

EMPATH

Someone who takes on other people's feelings as their own

ENERGETIC BOUNDARIES

Imagine if everyone walked around with a bubble around them. That's what your energy field looks like. Now imagine what happens when you stop to talk to somebody. Your bubbles touch for a period of time. When you and your conversation partner stay put, everything is fine, and the bubbles stay intact. But if your conversation partner comes closer to you than you feel comfortable with and you don't push away, then they keep on taking up your space, and eventually, your bubbles merge. Suddenly, it's not your bubble anymore, but a mix of yours and theirs!

This is where energetic boundaries come in. They are physical and spiritual barriers you place between yourself and the rest of the world so you can go about your day without getting drained by energy vampires (see definition) or losing a part of yourself.

ENERGETICS
The practice of moving divine energy to heal old wounds and blocked chakras and remove unhealthy attachments or cords. Reiki is probably the most popular study of energetics.

ENERGY CLEARING
A moment or a session to clear away negative energy and emotions using energetics. This can be done on your own or by an expert healer.

ENERGY VAMPIRES

Someone who is emotionally, mentally, physically, or spiritually demanding and high-maintenance. Any amount of time spent with an energy vampire will leave you feeling drained, irritated, and in need of being recharged.

FAITH

To step forward into the unknown and trust in the Divine that everything is as it should be

FREE WILL

The ability for humans to make their own choices, for their Highest Good or not

GENERATIONAL WOUNDS

Unresolved trauma, grudges, or limiting beliefs that have carried over from one generation of a family to the next

GROUNDING

Doing what you need to do to calm down, focus, and relax when you are in the face of overwhelm and confusion. In other words, "find solid ground." In the intuitive community, grounding yourself means realigning with the energy of the earth. Examples of grounding include taking a hike, walking barefoot outside, taking a nap, meditating, or journaling. These are all ways to ground your thoughts so you can come home to yourself instead of getting lost in the throes of everyone else's ideas and thoughts.

HEART SPACE

The area where your heart chakra resides—the chest. "Getting into your heart space" is the equivalent of "follow your heart."

HIGHLY SENSITIVE PERSON[3] (HSP)

The term "Highly-Sensitive Person" was first coined by Dr. Elaine Aron, a clinical psychologist who studies love and close relationships.

A Highly Sensitive Person is someone who is sensitive to sensory input (e.g., bright lights and loud noises) and notices little subtleties in whatever environment they encounter. Many traits of HSPs overlap with traits of empaths, so it can be confusing as to how to distinguish one from the other.

---

3   Elaine Aron, PhD, "The Highly Sensitive Person," https://hsperson.com/.

Just remember, the term "HSP" is related to physiology, and empathy is related to spiritual ability.

INTUITION
Internal wisdom attributed to the Higher Self or Spirit

LET GO OF WHAT NO LONGER SERVES YOU
This is a popular phrase used in the intuitive community. You will often see this in the personal development world too. The idea here is to look at all the areas of your life (e.g., health, relationships, finances) and prune away the issues that are causing you the most strife because they are no longer serving your Highest Good.

KARMA
The belief that every choice has energy and consequences. Choices that benefit yourself and others will create and manifest happiness and luck. Choices that result in harming others will result in harming yourself down the road.

KUNDALINI
Kundalini is described as the ultimate life force, much like a slithery serpent that lives at the base of the spine.

When it is activated, it goes from the spine, through the gut, then the heart and eventually the head to ignite all of the chakras. This concept has Buddhist and Hindu origins.

MANIFESTATION

The ability to make a desire, want, need, or wish into a reality with clear and focused intention. This was made famous by Abraham Hicks' version of the Law of Attraction (The Law of Attraction has been around since the 1800s, way before Abraham Hicks).

MEDITATION

The art of sitting still and being present. People practice meditation when they need to check in with themselves to reduce stress, let go of fear, and relax the mind just enough to let in new ideas and perspectives.

MESSAGES

These are messages sent from the Divine. They can take the form of downloads (see definition) or can be symbols from dreams, animals, numbers, cards, words, or memories. Oftentimes, if a message shows up more than once, there is great significance in it. Any resistance toward it won't make it go away. Instead, the messages will keep showing up until the person they were intended for acknowledges and accepts them.

Mind-Body-Spirit Alignment

This term is used to describe integrative medicine. When career, relationships, and dreams are all in line with what the mind, body, and spirit desire, then one can expect great health, abundance, joy, and prosperity with ease and grace.

Natal Chart

This is your astrology chart based on the day you were born, your place of birth and your time of birth. The natal chart provides information such as your sun sign, moon sign, rising, and all of the other houses and positions that were situated in space on the day you are born, which is believed to influence your gifts, your character, and your purpose.

Past Lives

This term directly relates to the idea of reincarnation: When we die, our souls leave our bodies and start all over again in a new body and new lifetime. The cycle continues over and over again. In each lifetime, the same soul is learning lessons and addressing past karma. Each life lived is considered a "past life." Whenever a person wants to find out who they were in the past, they will find an expert who specializes in akashic records or past life regression.

PSYCHIC

Oftentimes this term is associated with a "Miss Cleo" character, someone who is able to mysteriously see and know everything; this term is used to describe people who are intuitive and extra sensitive to their environment and the people around them. They are able to pick up on things faster and on a deeper level without being given any extra help. Sometimes this can pop up in the form of telepathy, clairvoyance (those who see visions), or clairsentience (those who just know).

QUANTUM

This term is used to describe going into realms outside of the 3D plane, where all desires can be brought into reality when declared in the quantum. It is widely believed that one only needs to tap into the quantum by relaxing their mind and diving deep into their spirit.

QUANTUM LEAPING

This is a term to describe a great amount of growth and momentum for someone within a short amount of time.

SHADOW WORK

Deeper spiritual work that involves facing one's shadow to get to the root cause of wounds and triggers in order to heal

SOULMATES

This used to be the primary accepted term for two people who are meant to be together. Nowadays, people use the term "Twin Flame" to explain people who are two halves of one whole and soulmates as people who resonate with you on a soul level. Soulmates don't have to be romantically entwined; the term can be familial or platonic. For instance, you can have friends who are soulmates because you are connected on such a deep soul level without any kind of "head over heels" love story.

SOURCE

God and the Divine. In other words, the source from where all creation is from.

SPIRIT

The Divine, whether it is God, spirit guides, or angels.

SPIRITUAL ALIGNMENT

Getting your mind, body, and spirit all on the same page, as opposed to compartmentalizing all of them into their own boxes

SPIRITUAL AWAKENING

The act of upleveling and a fuller realization of your spiritual world. Sometimes this can result in a state of confusion or physical sensations.

SURRENDER

Giving up control and expectation to surrender to God and the universe and trust in divine timing. Typically, this term is brought up when someone is going through a hard time, and all they can do is wish for a different outcome. But, when they surrender, they accept that they are where they need to be. It is believed that when you surrender, that is when the universe will move things in your favor.

TWIN FLAMES

Hollywood's preferred term is "soulmates." In the woo woo world, Twin Flames are two souls who split apart from one. Those who discover this theory often come across it because they suddenly felt a strong pull and attraction toward someone who they believe is their "Twin Flame." When you dive deeper into the Twin Flame journey, you come to learn that the journey is about unconditional self-love and accepting who you really are by coming into "union" with your soul. Many in the community believe that "union" means reuniting with the person who is your Twin Flame and living happily ever after. However, most leaders in the community agree that it is a journey for the Self and not a journey to be paired up.

UNCONDITIONAL LOVE

Love without conditions, grudges, or expectations. Oftentimes this is used within the community to refer to love for oneself (otherwise known as "self-love") or love for others, whether or not they are on good terms with you or not.

THE UNIVERSE

A colloquial for the combined force of God, spirit guides, and the power of the vibrations in everything (see Vibrations).

VIBRATIONS

Loosely based on String Theory, "vibrations" come from the idea that everything in the universe vibrates at certain frequencies, and those frequencies have the power to attract or repel the things you want. For instance, when something or someone is immersed in negativity, it is theorized that they are operating at a low frequency of vibration. Likewise, when someone is joyful and in pure exhilaration, they are functioning at a high frequency of vibration. The slang for vibrating at high frequencies is "high vibes."

WITCH

Once used to describe someone who was Wicca or practiced witchcraft, it is now a term used for people who follow similar rituals and incorporate them into their lifestyle. This includes using tarot cards, burning sage or palo santo, and honoring different moon cycles.

Download your free cheat sheet here!

Creatives

"My heart needs to be into it."

INSIDER'S LOOK

If your idea of a self-proclaimed "creative" is a Beatnik, snapping their fingers to signal approval or disapproval from a pretentious point of view, then I need you to put away this notion for a moment and listen up.

A "creative" is simply someone who loves to create. Period. Yes, it could be paintings, drawings, writings, or crafts, but it can include things you may not necessarily consider "creative," such as products, offers, services, programs, or even systems. This all stems from the love of self-expression and giving to those who are willing to receive this significant symbol of affection. In fact, I would even say the act of creating is even more important than the end product itself because it is about practicing the sacred ritual of the highest expression of the soul. From this lens, one can better understand that whatever a creative person spends their energy on needs to come from a personal place first. In other words, to get the green light to move forward on anything, the creative's heart needs to be all-in. There's no going around it. To deny this fact would mean denying who they really are at their core, and that is something that most of them have learned the hard way, to never betray.

Creatives are always coming up with ideas. In fact, they have ideas coming out of their ears! Feel free to blame it on their great love for ideals, passions, and big visions. When they are very engaged, you can expect to jump into deep experiential and philosophical discussions about everything and anything. I like to call them "rabbit holes."

STRENGTHS OF THIS **POPULATION**

NEED AN IDEA? THEY'VE GOT TWENTY!

Creatives are fantastic at brainstorming! In fact, brainstorming is quite possibly one of their top favorite pastimes, as it stirs up their creative juices. Plus, if you happen to be speaking to a creative who loves to help people, there is a double incentive here for them to engage in a brainstorming session with you. Think of them as walking and breathing muses, ready to evoke inspiration. If you are ever hitting a "writer's block" or an equivalent of it (because it doesn't always apply to writing), then be sure to have your phone list of trusted creative friends to talk it out with you for a quick idea-hashing session!

THEY LOVE THINKING OUTSIDE OF THE BOX.

Creatives naturally defy convention and question accepted paradigms. This applies to brainstorming, troubleshooting, and strategizing. This doesn't mean they actively break the rules (although I'm sure that accounts for some of the population). If you give them the set requirements and structure of whatever project you are working on, however, they will put on their thinking cap and find ideas and solutions that never crossed your mind before. They love taking something like a Rubik's Cube and looking at all 360 degrees in order to find many different possibilities! That's the key to all of this: finding opportunities and possibilities. This is the driver for many creatives.

THEY KNOW WHO THEY ARE.

Their core values, how they feel about different political issues, and their spiritual beliefs (if they have any) are usually pretty well-defined in this population. To embrace their self-expression, they have had to grow and accept who they are in all kinds of facets. The work they create is meant to be seen by the world. If they want their work to be seen, their internal work is preparing them to be seen by the world too.

THEY EMBRACE LOVE AND WONDER.

Here is one particular strength of creatives that should not go unnoticed: their ability to look at the fine details of something they deem beautiful (art, nature, love, or life) to learn and discover another aspect of themselves. I liken it to someone walking through an art gallery and stopping to observe a portrait of a beautiful woman. Aside from the central piece (the woman), they see the soft brush strokes of the trees behind her and the way the artist made the lake pop out from the background with the overall color palette and feel of the painting. By the end, the creative appreciates the painting at a deeper level and experiences internal growth in that very moment.

It's because of this ability that creatives are able to truly see something or someone in their glory and appreciate in ways that no one can imagine.

CHALLENGES FOR THIS POPULATION

BRAINSTORMING IS THEIR FRENEMY.

Brainstorming for other people is their wheelhouse! Brainstorming for themselves—that's a love-hate relationship. While creatives love to come up with new ideas, too much of anything is not good.

Back up for a second. One thing I always tell people is that it is hard to see ourselves. We are just too close to our own situations to see what is up and what is down. That's why you will more often see someone who is great at giving relationship advice but struggle with similar issues in their own relationships. They are too caught up in their emotions to see that the solution is right around the corner. They're not hypocrites; they are just too close to the issue at hand.

Now, going back to brainstorming for a creative, it's tough. An idea comes along, and it's love at first sight. Then another idea comes along, and the same "honeymoon" emotions rise up. Again and again, it keeps happening. The ideas eventually start to multiply into sub-ideas in an attempt to make sense of it all. Finally, when the creative gets a moment to breathe, a mounting pile of ideas has accumulated. Instead of seeing the many blessings, the creative sees one huge curse. The overwhelm is paralyzing because each idea represents a promise to themselves, and the longer they wait to fulfill these promises, the more shame and guilt they feel when it comes to their personal integrity. Do you see how this quickly snowballs into a vicious cycle?

That's why I call brainstorming the "frenemy" of the creative. Ideas are the first step in the creation process, the sole driver of a creative. Ideas are amazing and great! But too many of them is a heavy burden on the soul of the creative.

THEY HAVE A LOVE FOR CREATION BUT LESS SO FOR WHAT COMES AFTER.

It is easy for a creative to get excited about an idea, particularly if it suddenly popped into their head and then immediately felt driven to work on it. However, going after the kind of gratification that can only be achieved when the finish line is crossed can often be a source of frustration, particularly if it is a project that requires lots of details and logistics. This is especially true for business. Every business product and service begins with a fantastic idea and an inspired business owner. But many steps have to be taken in order to take that idea and turn it into something that will actually sell on the market. The idea needs to be validated, the end goal needs to be outlined, and a strategy needs to connect everything from start to finish. If a creative is not naturally inclined to look to structure and details for implementation, it makes it that much harder to hash out the real selling points of what they are creating, thus making it harder to finish the project—let alone get it properly ready to sell.

THEY'RE AT RISK OF STARTING TOO MANY THINGS AND NOT FINISHING THEM.

For creatives who have too many ideas, they are also at risk of starting too many projects at once with little to no help or resources. Their energy is scattered. Instead of focusing on one project at a time, their attention is spread out across many different projects. Progress is slow, and nothing gets done. Eventually, projects are competing like multiple siblings in a family trying to gain the attention of their parents. The feeling of overwhelm sets in, and eventually, it is difficult for the creative to know which project to focus on first.

MONEY GETS IN THE WAY.

Creatives consciously and unconsciously have a hard time creating something just for money. To create something, it needs to stem from their passion first and then find a way to make money. To ask a creative to make something without any emotional attachment to sell on the market would quickly deplete their creative juices, and eventually, the project feels more like a chore than something to be excited about. As Steven Pressfield said in his book *The War of Art*, "We must do our work for its own sake, not for fortune or attention or applause."[4]

The creative needs a container where they can fill their cup, revive their creative flow, and be free from the limits of money and everything that entails, or else creativity will devolve into an obligation. Without this, it is difficult for the creative to stay grounded and true to their path. Once the creative establishes a consistent habit to practice creativity liberally, then they are better able to take on money-making activities (e.g., sales calls, marketing, and pricing offers).

CREATIVES GET CAUGHT UP IN PERSONAL DOGMA.

Without a doubt, creatives are very much in tune with their ideals, beliefs, and core values. In fact, it is so heavily weaved within them that you could probably tell what their top three ideals are after speaking with them for twenty minutes. They know who they are, and they have found both subtle and obvious ways to make themselves known and seen by the world.

---

4   Steven Pressfield, *The War of Art: Break Through the Blocks and Win Your Inner Creative Battles* (New York: Black Irish Entertainment, LLC, 2012), 161.

There may be topics that fire a creative's passion or emotion so much that it activates fiery rhetoric. When this happens, it can be hard to get a word in edgewise as they dominate the conversation, and, depending on the person or situation, they can be easily triggered or reactive to opposing views.

THEY ARE VULNERABLE TO RESISTANCE.

Ever heard of "writer's block"? Yep! That's resistance! In fact, I have hit resistance many times in writing this book. Steven Pressfield put it best, touching on resistance for the entirety of his book, *The War of Art*:

> "Resistance is experienced as fear; the degree of fear equates to the strength of Resistance. Therefore, the more fear we feel about a specific enterprise, the more certain we can be that that enterprise is important to us and to the growth of our soul. That's why we feel so much Resistance. If it meant nothing to us, there'd be no Resistance."[5]

This is part of building the hunger and the humility to become a great artist; HOWEVER, it is a battle that

---

5   Pressfield, *The War of Art*, 39.

has to be waged and faced multiple times in every creative endeavor. It is not for the faint of heart, and many have left projects unfinished when they fall victim to resistance.

THEY STRUGGLE WITH THE CURSE OF INFINITE POSSIBILITIES.

Nothing is more paralyzing than looking in the face of infinite possibilities, especially when there is no inclination to go one way over another. This often occurs when a creative experiences big chunks of free time and has too many ideas to prioritize. While they know full-well that forward action of any kind can relieve their burden, it still does nothing for alleviating the pressure building up inside. Life is short, and they need to seize the opportunity to make big things happen. And yet, they still can't bring themselves to move. It is a slow crawl to death, and it is frightening.

WHAT THE CONVERSATION STARTER NEEDS TO KEEP IN MIND

YOUR SELF-EXPRESSION IS A MUST.

When speaking to creatives who thrive on self-expression, you need to first understand how you express who you are. Is it in your words? The clothes you wear? The symbols you often reference and hold in reverence? When you are finding common ground with a creative, you need to understand who you are and how you project that to the world because chances are, the creative is already piecing that together in their head all throughout your initial conversation and thereafter. In other words, understand who you are and be you.

CREATIVES LOVE EXPANSIVE THINKING WITHOUT LIMITS.

Remember how I said creatives love to come up with ideas and start things? It all comes from the love of thinking bigger and connecting the dots. To have a conversation that is all about coming up with new ways to embark on new endeavors is fun, relaxing, and quite exciting for the creative.

But asking them to prioritize some ideas over others and add structure to them can feel deflating and constrictive. That's why the creative needs to be in the right mindset to receive advice or feedback for their ideas. They have to want to shave things down and fully understand that sometimes this is what it takes to get things done. Therefore, please wait until a creative asks for your feedback on their ideas—particularly the ones they are extremely excited about.

HELP THEM FILL THEIR CUPS.

No one has it easy, no matter who you are, because that's life. For the creatives who find themselves in a place where they are burned out and have little time to themselves, their first love goes out the window: the ability to create.

It's a catch-22, really. They need to create to fill their cups, but they need their cups filled in order to create something. When I'm tapped out from juggling my business and my role as a mom and a wife, it is super hard for me to write for myself because I have nothing left, even though I know writing would help me feel better.

When you are speaking to a creative and they clearly express that their cup is empty, they are looking for some kindling to light their fires. Now, this doesn't mean you force them to sit in front of a blank canvas to paint. No. In fact, the best thing you can do is show them compassion and find a way to get them excited about their art again. For instance, you can talk about how much they have helped you in the past with gaining new insights and what that meant to you. You can also bring up one of their past projects to remind them what their personal mission is. Essentially, talk about their gifts to remind them of their life purpose. You'd be surprised how much perspective you can give them just by doing this.

CREATIVES VALUE CHARACTER OVER KNOWLEDGE.

Knowledge is power, but character trumps it when a creative is around. It doesn't matter if you are able to recite a whole encyclopedia like the back of your hand or have a bunch of letters after your name. If you have a wall up around your heart and give no inclination as to who you authentically are, then no creative is going to give you the time of day.

RECOMMENDED COMMUNICATION STRATEGIES

OFFER TO HELP BRAINSTORM OR CREATE STRUCTURE.

It is hard for any of us to see ourselves because we are too close. Offering to give them structure for their end goal is super helpful! They may be great at helping other people with their structure, but they may have a hard time coming up with practical plans for their own projects.

When invited, clarity is a gift. But you have to be invited first!

GEEK OUT ON PARTICULAR TOPICS.

When you converse with a creative, if you find out that the two of you share a common interest, then seize this opportunity to geek out with them. Talk about the finer details and slowly watch as they follow your lead. As you go back and forth, notice what begins to take place: a secret camaraderie for which only a few select people know the hidden passcode. Plus, you will have a ton of fun in the process.

SHARE THE LATEST CREATIVE PROJECTS WITH EACH OTHER.

Now, I know what you are thinking. This looks A LOT like the point I just made about "geeking out" on a topic. Well, guess what? It's not the same! My last point hinged on finding a topic that you and your conversation partner had a shared experience and passion for.

For this point, I'm suggesting sharing whatever creative endeavors you have on your plate. They can be any topic, on any platform, with any modality. Allow your conversation partner to share what they are currently working on and ask them all about it. You will most likely learn something new, and your vested interest will excite your conversation partner. Once you are done speaking about their project, switch roles by talking about what you're working on. The point of this exercise is to share in the love of creation, and you can't do that when the conversation is one-sided.

SHARE WHAT YOU ARE PASSIONATE ABOUT.

If you are having trouble breaking the ice or finding a middle ground with a new creative acquaintance, start with what you're passionate about. It doesn't matter if they are passionate about the same thing. It is a good start because every single person on this planet is passionate about something, and that alone is a great conversation opener. Plus, once you talk about what you're passionate about, then that gives the other person a good idea as to what your core values are and invites them to talk about what they are passionate about too.

APPRECIATION IS ALWAYS APPRECIATED.

Support in the form of gratitude and appreciation is always welcomed. If your creative friend shows you something they made, tell them how inspired you are by their work and attention to detail. Or if they performed a service utilizing their creative gifts, tell them how it was helpful for you and thank them. Positive reinforcement is always a great thing, as long as it is real and genuine. No faking it 'till you make it! That's not how you build real relationships!

ARTISTS HAVE BRAINS, TOO.

If you meet someone who considers herself an "artist," don't ever assume she can't have an intellectual conversation with you. Many artisans are well-versed in their craft and lived many lives. You cannot predict a person's IQ, and it would be unwise to judge someone based on how smart you perceive they are. Just remember there are different kinds of intelligence and when you meet a creative, always give them the benefit of the doubt. If you are speaking about a topic that they are not familiar with, don't balk at how they should know more about the subject. Instead, take it as an opportunity to teach them something new with compassion and vigor. They will leave the conversation feeling respected, and you will have created a space where you got to be heard.

TELL YOUR STORY.

It should come as no surprise to anyone that I would mention this as a communication strategy. After all, my business is called Untold Story Enterprises! Stories have the power to connect people emotionally because they allow the listener to see a 360-degree view of the storyteller. When you tell your story honestly and from the heart, you allow the other person to see a bit of your soul, and if they like what they see, they will keep that door open.

EMBRACE SYMBOLS AND METAPHORS.

If you have a lucky charm or a special symbol that has a sentimental meaning, share it. The power of symbols, talismans, and metaphors is as ancient as the human race and is often a reminder of things we hold dear. They can also give someone a bird's eye view of your core beliefs and values. Since creatives are very grounded in their values, they would especially love going down conversational rabbit holes regarding symbols and metaphors.

DON'T HESITATE TO USE THE POWER OF MUSIC.

If all else fails, go with another universal language: music. The majority of people listen to music, and one can choose from a plethora of genres to chat about. This is a pretty safe door opener. Take heed, though; if you or the person you are speaking to is judgmental when it comes to music, then tread softly.

KEYWORDS AND KEY PHRASES

ART
Any form of expression, whether that's poetry, painting, drawing, sculpting, dance, writing, or anything else one can think of

BRAIN DUMP
The act of unloading all of an individual's ideas from their head to a piece of paper or a person

BRAINSTORM
The act of coming up with more ideas, namely when an individual is "stuck"

CRAFT

A skill that reflects the individual's workmanship and years of dedication to learn and practice

CREATIVITY

The ability and the drive to create

GIFT

Special abilities that all of us have naturally, sometimes since birth. This can be in the form of a skill such as writing, acting, or sewing. Or it can be a practice that is conducted consciously or unconsciously. Gifts are something we do particularly well and excel at without too much energy or notice.

INSPIRATION

The sudden onset of clarity coupled with the urge to take action to go after an idea or dream

MUSE

A common archetype from which inspiration is birthed. Originating from the nine Muses in Greek Mythology who helped to inspire men and women with poetry, song, and art.

RESISTANCE

Steven Pressfield's overarching umbrella term that encompasses "blocks," "writers' blocks," or "loss of inspiration, clarity, and motivation." The internal shadow or blockage that keeps an artist or creative from moving forward on their best and highest work. This may take the form of writer's block or procrastination.

WRITER'S BLOCK

When a writer is having a hard time concentrating on their writing projects and cannot get the words out of his/her head and onto paper. See Resistance.

Download your free cheat sheet here!

Analytical Thinkers

"It just needs to make sense."

INSIDER'S LOOK

Often a misunderstood population, analytical thinkers are known for their brains and their love for data and structure. The reason why they are often "misunderstood" is because their love for facts, numbers, and figures has become a language all on its own and is often beyond what other people are able or willing to comprehend.

When it comes to ideas and project design, they often look to proven processes heavily backed up by extensive research in order to increase their likelihood for significant success and results. Needless to say, when debating an analytical thinker, you will need to present proper evidence, data, and social proof to substantiate your point. Analytical thinkers conduct thorough research before committing to a new project. Processes and standard operating procedures are valued like gold because they keep everything linear and moving in a consistent and systematic manner. They highly value credibility, integrity, reputation, and experience when it comes to people they work with or people they look to as advisors or mentors. This means presenting the projects you've worked on, the results of those projects, how many years you've worked in the industry, and how many degrees you have achieved.

STRENGTHS OF THIS POPULATION

THE "HOW" IS AS EASY AS CAKE.

For those of you who have an easy time dreaming up the vision behind your WHY but have difficulty with figuring out "the how" to make it all work practically, have no fear. This is where analytical thinkers come in to save the day. Analytical thinkers have a way of understanding complicated concepts, breaking them down into smaller bite-sized details, and piecing them together into an actionable plan. They create realistic structure when most people would rather avoid it like the plague. If you are building a team for your business or organization, you should definitely consider recruiting at least one or two strong analytical thinkers. You'll thank me later.

Simon Sinek referenced this same point in his famous book *Start With Why*. Sinek says:

> WHY-TYPES have the power to change the course of industries or even the world...if only they knew HOW. WHY-types are the visionaries, the ones with the overactive imaginations. They tend to be optimists who believe that all the things they imagine can actually be accomplished. HOW-types live more in the here and now. They are realists and have a clearer sense of all things practical. WHY-types are focused on the things most people can't see, like the future. HOW-types are focused on things most people can see and tend to be better at building structures and processes and getting things done. One is not better than the other; they are just different ways people naturally see and experience the world. [Bill] Gates is a WHY-type. And Steve Jobs. And Herb Kelleher. But

they didn't do it alone. They couldn't. They needed those who knew HOW.[6]

THEY LOVE CONNECTING THE DOTS FOR SUCCESS.

While some people want to create something on a whim or because it sounded like a great idea to them, analytical thinkers approach things in a way that is based on results. In other words, they are more likely to think of the end result first, then create something by working backward. Instead of creating an online course because they suddenly felt the need to create it, they would first look at their end goal. In this hypothetical example, the end goal would be to make $10K in passive income. Then they would construct a product and a funnel that would directly feed into the $10K passive income goal. Their ultimate objective is to make sure they have a clear pathway to go from start to finish while keeping all hypothetical outcomes in mind.

---

6   Simon Sinek, Start With Why: How Great Leaders Inspire Everyone to Take Action (New York: Portfolio, 2001), page 139].

THEY HAVE APPRECIATION AND RESPECT FOR CREATING STRUCTURES, PROCESSES, AND SYSTEMS.

Analytical thinkers appreciate and highly value efficiency, resourcefulness, ingenuity, consistency, and proven processes. Structures, processes, and systems have built-in safeguards to reduce error rates and allow for production to be duplicatable. Rinse. Repeat. Rinse. Repeat. Things run like clockwork and allow the end user to scale their projects, products, and services.

ANALYTICALS CONDUCT INDEPENDENT RESEARCH AND STUDIES TO FORMULATE OPINIONS.

Everyone has an opinion. Thus, it should come as no surprise that analytical thinkers are full of them too. While I can't speak for all analyticals, I have noticed a trend among the majority: As opposed to stating their opinion after hearing about a new discovery from one source, they will reserve judgment while researching a topic from many different sources. They expect to encounter biases and consequently read with a healthy level of skepticism. After they have gathered enough data, they will finally make their opinion known to the world. They do this to stay as grounded and objective as possible. This is a key piece of their integrity.

CHALLENGES FOR THIS POPULATION

THEY ENCOUNTER DIFFICULTY WITH DISTINGUISHING EXPERTISE AND TRUST-BUILDING.

This is something I have seen in the sciences, in digital marketing, in programmers, and in the financial industry. The experts I have observed in these industries all tend to recite their titles and resumes as elevator pitches and greeting cards. While expertise is definitely important when defending your work and showing credibility, too much of an emphasis on it creates detachment and inhibits connection with people not in their industry. In other words, if you are an analytical thinker and you speak ONLY about your expertise to someone who is not in your industry or thinks very differently than you, then you stand to lose their attention and miss the opportunity to establish trust.

Remember, establishing expertise is a different bucket from building trust. Don't try to compile them both into the same container. It just doesn't work.

THEIR INDUSTRY LANGUAGE CAN INHIBIT THEM FROM CONNECTION.

Sometimes their analytical thinking and their industry knowledge blend so well together, it becomes their main language for communicating with everyone in their personal and professional circles. In turn, it is difficult for them to turn it off when they are around people who are not analytical thinkers or members of the same industry and, as a result, sound esoteric and alien. When people cannot understand you, they cannot connect with the message you are trying to convey. That's why this challenge often manifests as difficulty with keeping people's attention or striking up conversations.

ANALYTICAL THINKERS ARE OFTEN MISUNDERSTOOD.

Communicating complex or high-level concepts in a way that is understandable can be challenging for analytical thinkers, particularly when they are speaking to people who can't picture what they are talking about. As hard as these analytical thinkers try to communicate these things as best they can, a lot of times people still don't understand it. This often leaves the analytical thinker feeling undervalued and unheard.

WHAT THE CONVERSATION STARTER
NEEDS TO KEEP IN MIND

This population is looking for structure, common sense, logic, results, proven processes, and deliverables. Anytime you work with an analytical thinker, as a client or teammate, you need to deliver what you say you do, make a fair and valid argument for it before work has begun, and follow through once work begins.

RECOMMENDED
COMMUNICATION STRATEGIES

Ask about their origins.

Find out what they studied in school and talk about it at length with them. This is your opportunity to ask them why they got into their profession and how they got started. Don't be surprised if you see a change in their body language and feel a shift in the air. Asking someone about their "why" will always draw out a response from a deeper place than the normal "who," "what," "where," and "how." In fact, I would even say the "why" is so profoundly foundational that it almost opens up a window into someone's heart and soul, no matter who they are.

ASK THEM ABOUT SPREADSHEETS AND DATA.

Stay with me here. Spreadsheets are more than grids, tables, and formulas. They are a way to see and manipulate data in plain view to discover the hidden story behind the numbers. If you're speaking with an analytical thinker, chances are they have a special relationship with data and spreadsheets.

When you do ask them about spreadsheets and data, make sure there is context. It would be awkward to suddenly ask someone, "Do you like spreadsheets?" when there is nothing leading up to it. Now, if the person you're talking to starts talking about keeping track of numbers to find the answer to this one question they were dying to solve, then that's the time to start asking questions.

SHARE SOME KNOWLEDGE.

Share an interesting study or statistic having to do with the topic at hand or their expertise, BUT be prepared to be asked for specifics (e.g., "Which study did you get this information from?" or "What was the sample size?")

With this crowd, you can't just say, "I Googled it and saw this on some random site or saw it on social media." They want to see that you are an objective thinker who will do their due diligence to research any findings you come across.

BRING UP YOUR IDEAS.

Share your ideas with them but be ready for questions pertaining to the end goal, the structure, and the little details.

Coming to the conversation with a prepared structure will show an analytical who you really are and what you have planned and also show them that you are not "all over the place."

Doing something based on a whim or a sudden burst of emotions won't have any clout with analytical thinkers. In fact, they are likely more occupied with finding the logical reasoning behind a project and will be too distracted to follow along and eventually will lose interest.

TRY TELLING STORIES.

Analytical thinkers can appreciate stories too, but when you're trying to prove a point, it is best to have numbers and data from a reputable source to back you up!

KEYWORDS AND KEY PHRASES

ALGORITHM

A set of rules, processes, or instructions for computations and calculations. Often, you'll see this in computers, apps, social media, the Rubik's Cube, or good old-fashioned mathematics.

DATA

A set of information yielded or generated from experiments, processes, or systems that, when analyzed, will yield answers

DELIVERABLE

What will be produced at the end of a service or process

METRICS

Units of measurements to assess something quantitatively

PARAMETERS
A predetermined set of conditions to define what is within and outside the scope of an experiment, process, idea, system, or program

PROOF OF CONCEPT
Evidence and results-in-hand to show that something is a success

PROVEN PROCESS
A process that has been perfected over time through much trial and error and now has enough evidence to usually give guaranteed results

PROCESS
A series of steps designed to yield a specific result

RESULTS
The product of an experiment, study, assessment, or research

RESEARCH
When broken down, this word is all about "searching" for answers over and over (RE-search). It's not enough to hear Sally state a fact she heard from someone else.

Research involves directly looking up sources to find clues to the answers the user seeks.

STRUCTURE

The skeleton for an idea to make it tangible and realistic

SYSTEMS

A container where processes flow from one to another, from start to finish, to produce a product or result. They can be "closed" or "open."

SPREADSHEETS

These are electronic documents full of vertical and horizontal gridlines where the user can input data and analyze it using different formulas and functions. Oftentimes these are used to sort out ideas and record information. You can easily find spreadsheets in Google Sheets and Microsoft® Excel.

Download your free cheat sheet here!

What All Three Have in Common

If you've made it this far, congratulations! You've made your way through a TON of material, and you deserve a pat on the back for that!

Whether you've taken it upon yourself to memorize some of the concepts or terms in this book or just mildly skimmed through as needed, here is what I want you (the reader) to take away:

> How we communicate is more of a reflection of our life experiences and our gifts rather than our divides and differences.

That's why I say that as different as these three populations are, they are all very much the same too.

When you engage all three populations, they will naturally go down rabbit holes and develop a deep loyalty to you. Most of all, they all want to be heard and seen for who they are without judgment.

More of us are on the same page than you can ever imagine. We're just speaking different languages. If we can recognize that, we can change the world. Literally, figuratively, and linguistically.

References

Aron, Elaine, PhD. "The Highly Sensitive Person." Accessed January 13, 2022. https://hsperson.com/.

Chopra, Deepak. "Deepak Chopra Explains the Law of Karma." *The Joy Within*. Written January 20, 2020. https://thejoywithin.org/authors/deepak-chopra/the-law-of-karma#:~:text=Deepak%20Chopra%20Karma%2C%20when%20properly%20understood%2C%20is%20just,the%20mechanics%20through%20which%20consciousness%20manifests.%20Deepak%20Chopra.

Lindberg, Sara. "What Are The 7 Chakras and How Can You Unblock Them?" *Healthline*. Written August 24, 2020. https://

www.healthline.com/health/what-are-chakras#the-7-main-chakras.

Miller, Katie. "What is Ayurveda?" *WebMD*. Written March 20, 2021. https://www.webmd.com/balance/guide/ayurvedic-treatments#1.

Ra M, Aline. "Kundalini Energy: What It Is and How To Awaken It Within You." *Medium*. Written February 27, 2020. https://medium.com/mindfully-speaking/kundalini-energy-what-it-is-and-how-to-awaken-it-within-you-a542f8aa39ed.

About the Author

Amy Lanci loves finding the gold within people. As a second generation Chinese American, Amy was born and raised in the Los Angeles county area of southern California. As a young girl, she was speech-delayed and quite scared of the world. Despite nine years of speech therapy, she remained awkward and shy for the rest of her childhood. Along the way, she discovered a love for writing that took the form of fictional stories and journal writing and a love for marine biology. After earning her undergraduate degree in ecology, behavior and evolution from the University of California, San Diego, she began her career in sea turtle genetics as a contractor for the Marine Turtle Genetics Program at the Southwest Fisheries Science Center as an employee for Ocean Associates, Inc.

Although everything seemed okay from the outside, the inside was a much different story. Amy struggled with her weight, her emotional eating, and her ability to establish boundaries to protect her sensitive nature. Finally, at the age of twenty-four, Amy was pushed to finally work on her personal issues when she was diagnosed with non-alcoholic fatty liver disorder. She finally worked on her emotional eating, lost weight, healed her liver, and found her husband.

When she looked at her journey and her career, she decided to try something new. At first, she got certified as a health coach from the Institute for Integrative Nutrition (IIN) and started her first business. After two years, the health coaching practice went nowhere and she was at a loss. Her then-business coach, Tiffany Largie, challenged her to switch over her business to copywriting and communication. Within a week of changing over her website and her business cards to reflect this new direction, Amy got her first two paying clients ever.

"It was as if the Universe was telling me, 'Go that way!'"

While juggling her responsibilities as a wife and mother, Amy worked hard to build her business during her off-hours in order to pursue her dream. Every time she spoke on stage and presented her story, she was constantly reminded of what her gifts were and how she straddled the line between intuition, creativity, and being analytical. It was the path to becoming whole.

After the sudden death of her dear friend and coach, KeeKee Cornelious, Amy finally found the courage to jump fully into entrepreneurship. Eight days after receiving the sad news of KeeKee's death, Amy sent in her three-month notice and wrapped up her fourteen-year career in science.

Now she is on a mission to make sure she uses her gifts to help people translate their dreams into words to make sure they are heard.

Are you having trouble describing "what you do" to your audience? Book a strategy call here to learn how to start speaking your audiences' language!

https://bit.ly/strategycallwithamy